Total System

How to Jump 8"-14" Higher or More

And Increase Your Speed, Endurance, and Stamina

By Trevor Thomas

Copyright © 2018
All rights reserved.
ISBN-13: 9781726784320
ISBN: 1726784320

Disclaimer:

This report is written for informational purposes only. The author has made every effort to make sure the information is complete and accurate, up to the publishing date. This report should be used in the making of an informed decision only. The publisher and author shall have neither liability nor responsibility to any person or entity with respect to any loss or damage caused or alleged to be caused directly or indirectly by this report.

As with any fitness activity involving repetitive motion, there is always the possibility of injury to the athlete such as muscle pulls or strained ligaments or tendons. Therefore, we assume no responsibility or liability in the event that injury does occur to the athlete during the use of this program.

This book is copyright 2018 with all rights reserved. It is illegal to copy, distribute, or create derivative works from this book in whole or in part or to contribute to the copying, distribution, or creating of derivative works of this book. If you try to copy, steal, or distribute all or any part of this book without permission, I will have my attorney contact you and make you wish that you'd never had such a stupid idea in your life. Count on it. By purchasing this book, you agree to the following: You understand that the information contained on this page and in this book is an opinion, and it should be used for personal entertainment purposes only. You are responsible for your own behavior, and none of this book is to be considered legal or personal advice. And I expect you to abide by these rules. I regularly and actively search the Internet for people who violate my copyrights. Total Jump System ©2018, All Rights Reserved. Now let's learn about how to increase your vertical jump.

Table of Contents

Introduction 5

Chapter 1: Goal Planning 7

Chapter 2: Preparing 9

Chapter 3: Equipment Needed.............................. 11

Chapter 4: The System 14

    Warming Up 15

    Stretching 17

    Exercises 21

    Optional Exercises 31

    Cooling Down 33

Chapter 5: Measuring Progress 34

Conclusion 36

Total Jump System Workout Chart.......................... 37

Total Jump System Progress Chart 38

INTRODUCTION

Welcome to the Total Jump System. This program is designed to make you an overall better athlete. Not only will it help you jump higher, but it will also increase your endurance, speed, stamina, and muscle strength. There are a total of six exercises associated with the program, as well as some warm-up exercises, stretching, and optional exercises to help with sprinting.

The program lasts a total of 15 weeks and you will maintain 95% of the results as long as you maintain active in your sport. The program works by using habitual jump training. The science behind habitual jump training is it works specific muscles in your legs, muscles that you use when you jump, more than most people have ever worked them before. When you play a sport, you may use these leg muscles, but you do not come close to working them like this program does. And by specifically focusing on these muscles each week, you get them to work harder, get stronger, and grow bigger, which all equals you jumping higher than ever before.

The workout chart and progress chart are located on the final pages of this book.

***Note: I wrote this book in an effort to help athletes become better athletes and excel at their sport. Reviews on Amazon are the backbone of books. If this book has helped you, please leave a 5 star review on Amazon. If for any reason you are not satisfied with this book, before leaving any type of negative review on Amazon, please email me at trevor@unknownwealth.com so we can work out a resolution.

Chapter 1: Goal Planning

For this program to work, you have to set goals you can obtain. So get out a piece of paper, and define the goals you want to accomplish using the Total Jump System. Are you trying to jump higher? Run faster? Have more endurance? A combination of all three? Set fulfilling, but realistic and obtainable goals. And remember, the most important aspect to achieving these goals is a strong belief in yourself.

There are three things you must do for this program to work... practice, practice, practice. For this program to work, you're going to have to use it and practice what it teaches. Once you begin the program and start seeing results, you will be more motivated to reach the goals you set for yourself. No one can accomplish the goals you set or make you do this program except for yourself! So you have to motivate and rely on yourself to succeed.

The science behind the Total Jump System is based on repetition and habitual jump training. As you do the exercises more and more, this system teaches the muscles in your legs to jump higher and higher. And the great part about this program is it's very convenient; it can be done anywhere as it uses only your own body weight and common items that can be found around your house. This means no bulky, expensive shoes, weights, or gym equipment is necessary. You can also do this program by yourself or with others for more motivation. The program lasts a total of 15 weeks.

Chapter 2: Preparing

There are a few things you must do in order to prepare for this program and get your body prepped for the best possible results. The first thing to do to prepare your body is maintain a healthy diet with good eating habits. You want to make sure to eat plenty of protein, carbohydrates, and drink plenty of water.

Protein

Protein is essential for muscle growth and bigger muscles means more jumping power. Professional body builders typically eat their body weight in grams of protein. While this isn't necessary for this program, you do want to increase your protein intake as this will help your leg muscles grow stronger. I suggest using a whey protein powder, as it's the cheapest and quickest way to get a large amount of protein.

Carbohydrates

Carbs give you the energy you need to do the system the best you can. Examples of foods filled with carbohydrates are fruits, vegetables, cereal, and bread. Most people get plenty of carbs, so you shouldn't have to worry too much about this.

Water

Water is not a nutrient but is needed in every part of the body to function. Water helps with many, many processes in the body and you can't get too much of it, especially when you are training and working out. So stop with the soda and other sugary drinks and drink more water!

Make sure to eat at least 1-2 hours before each work out, as this will give you the necessary energy to give you the results you want. Another good idea is to get 7-9 hours of sleep each night so you won't be falling asleep during your workout.

As stated before, the program lasts a total of 15 weeks and the exercises are done five days a week, with 2 days off for resting your muscles. Consistency is another big thing so really try to do this program at the same time each day. This will give you the best results and make it easier to remember to do your workout each day.

Chapter 3: Equipment Needed

Basketball Shoes or Sneakers

Basketball or Volleyball

Chair

Thick Book or Stair Steps or Stairs

This program is highly effective because it focuses on the primary muscles in your legs that are used when jumping. The secret to the program is it trains your legs naturally to jump. The program concentrates on muscles in your thighs, upper calves, lower calves, and Achilles tendons. And what makes it great is your body weight is the only resistance needed.

Now in the first five days you start this program, you will notice a decrease in your vertical jump due to sore muscles, as well as new muscle use. You should be able to start seeing an increase in your jump on about the 7th day.

Chapter 4: The System

There are a total of six exercises associated with this program, 2 more optional exercises, as well as warming up, cooling down, and stretching techniques. Use the workout chart (located on the last pages of the book) for the specific number of repetitions and sets to be done per week.

Key Terms:

Repetition – completing one motion of an exercise; also called a "rep".

Set – repeating a repetition a continuous number of times to complete a cycle.

Warming Up

These exercises are designed to increase blood circulation and loosen up muscles before your workout. They also prevent muscle pulls and strained tendons & ligaments. You're basically just getting your body ready for the workout. You can do either one of these exercises, just make sure to perform the exercise you choose for 3-5 minutes.

Jog in Place

Jumping Jacks

1 2 3 4

Stretching

Stretching is essential after warming up because it helps prevent muscle pulls, strains and cramps. For all the stretches below, after completing the stretch for one leg, switch legs and stretch the other.

Calf Stretch

First you're going to stretch your calves. To do this, place the ball of your foot on the edge of a stair, thick book, or cinder block, and let your heel hang over the edge. Use a railing or chair to hold onto for support.

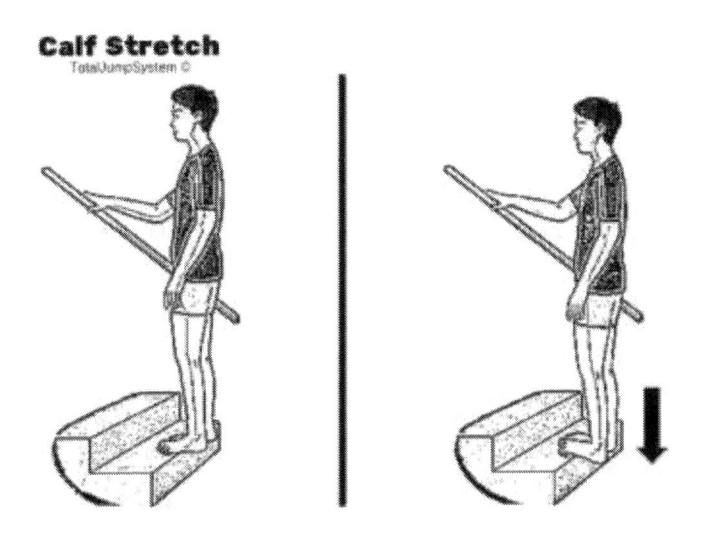

Thigh Stretch

Next you want to stretch your thighs. To do this, stand straight up and bend the leg you wish to stretch behind you; then pull the elevated ankle of that leg behind you upward.

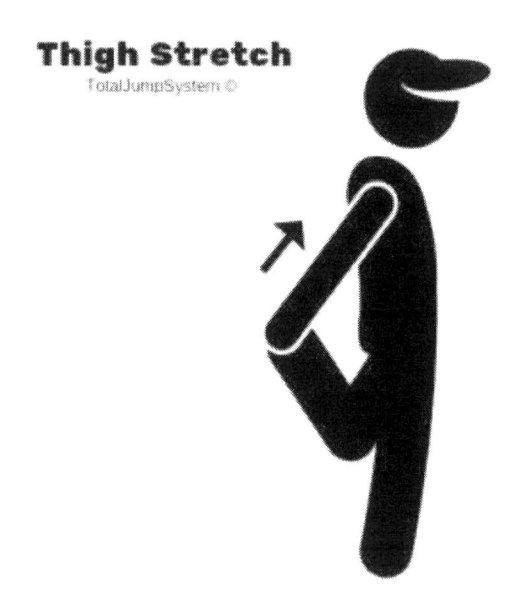

Hamstring Stretch

After this you are going to want to stretch your hamstring. To do this, place the heel of the leg you wish to stretch on a chair. While keeping the other leg firmly planted on the floor, lean your body toward the elevated knee.

Lower Back Stretch

Next stretch your lower back. To do this, lie flat on your back, and while placing your hands under your knees, pull your bent legs into your chest.

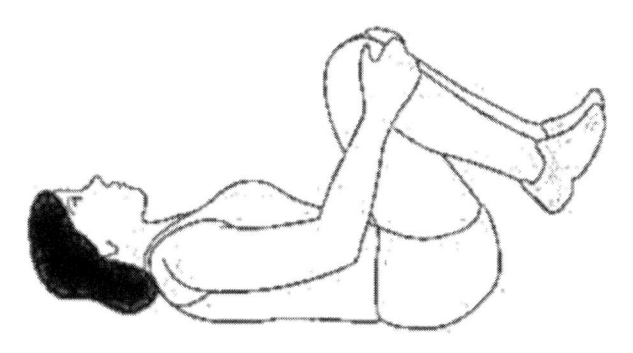

Note: In all the stretching exercises, hold the stretch for at least 20 seconds where you feel the most tension.

The Exercises

The Total Jump System consists of six exercises, as well as two optional exercises.

Hop-Ups

Hop-ups are one of the best exercises for increasing your vertical jump because they target muscles in your thighs that initially thrust you up. Hop-ups also help with endurance and stamina. Hop-ups are a modified version of jumping rope, so they are a little bit easier if done with a jump rope, but if you don't have one they can be done without it.

While looking straight ahead, keep your hands at your side and jump 10-12" off the ground. Make sure to always land on the balls of your feet (the part of your foot closet to your toes) and then bend your legs into a quarter squat position, which is between sitting and standing. You will feel your thigh muscles working and burning. Then repeat.

Hop Ups
TotalJumpSystem ©

1 2 3 4

Rest 3-4 minutes between sets.

Here is a video showing hop ups in action:
https://goo.gl/2ZBL3m

Calf Raises

Strong calves are very important for finishing your jump. For this exercise you'll need a thick book, cinder block, or stair step. Use a chair, bar or stair rail for balance. While standing straight up, place the ball (front of foot) of one foot on the block and let the heal hang over the edge. The other foot will be bent 90 degrees and elevated. Your entire body weight will be resting on your planted foot.

Next raise yourself up on your toes as high as you can using only your calf muscle, then lower yourself back down so your heel is below the edge of what you're standing on.

Calf Raises

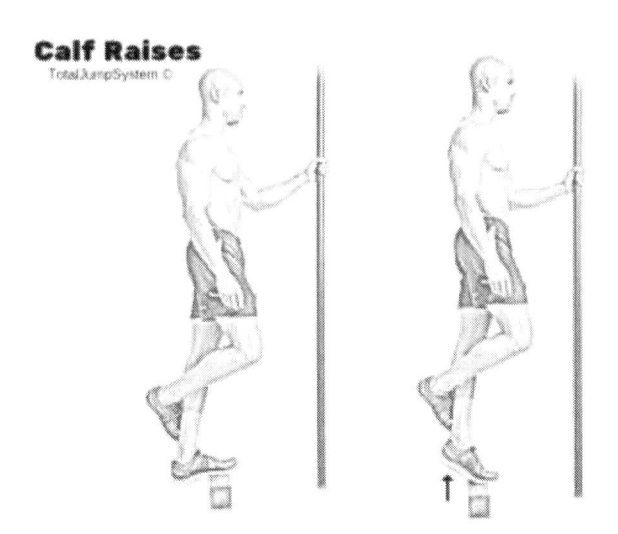

When you complete the reps for one calf, duplicate the exercise with the other calf. Working both calves completes 1 set; rest 25 seconds between sets.

Here is a video showing calf raises in action:
https://goo.gl/t7vkhz

Step-Ups

Step-ups are a great exercise for strengthening your thighs and developing single leg jumping power. For this exercise you'll need a sturdy chair. Place the chair in front of you and put one foot on the chair so your thigh is parallel to the ground. You should be in a stepping position with one foot flat on the chair and one foot flat on the floor.

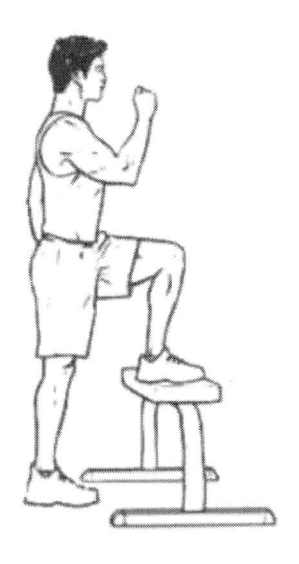

To begin the exercise, push up with the elevated foot as hard as you can so that your foot actually leaves the chair. When you're in the air, switch legs so that when you land you're in the opposite position as you were before. Repeat with the other leg to complete one repetition.

Step Ups

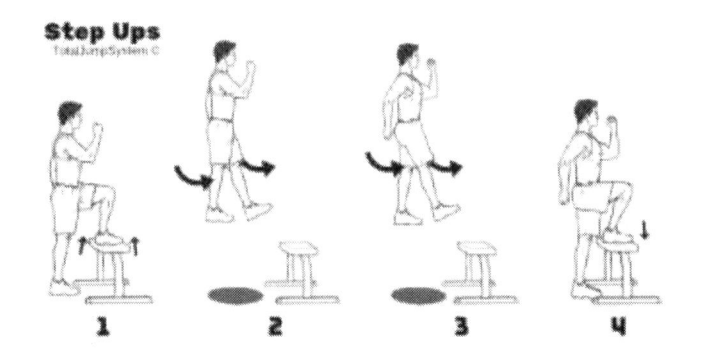

Rest 3-4 minutes in between sets.

Here is a video showing step ups in action:
https://goo.gl/do5mF1

Spring Ups

Spring Ups are designed to strengthen your calves, the sides of your thighs, and your Achilles tendons. This exercise develops quick explosive jumping power. To begin, stand straight up and jump or thrust yourself up as high as you can. Then the split second that you land, jump back up as hard and as high as possible trying not to bend your legs. You may use your arms to propel yourself back up.

Rest 1 minute in between sets.

Here is a video showing spring ups in action: https://goo.gl/1DYwkp

Jumpouts

Jumpouts are quick type jumps designed to strengthen the high end of your calf muscles. To begin the exercise, stand on your tip toes as high as possible. Begin jumping repeatedly, no more than 1 inch off the ground. Land only on your tip toes and jump back up to 1 inch, keeping your legs straight the entire time.

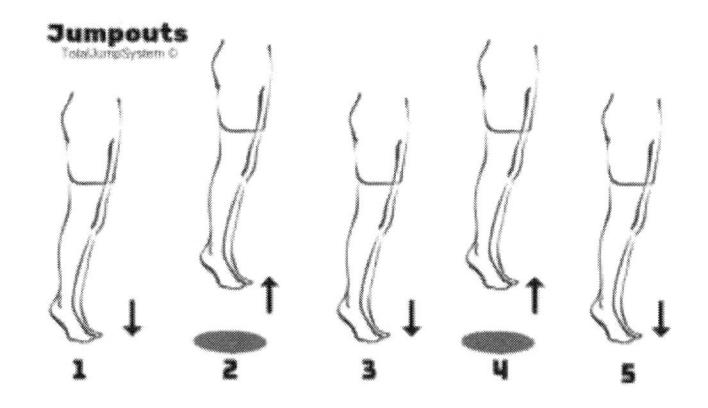

Here is a video of Jumpouts in action: https://goo.gl/TiZoTn

Squat Hops

For balance, hold a basketball or volleyball at chest level. You can hold the ball by either putting your hands on each side it, or by hugging it. Next, while holding the ball, squat down into a sitting position. Make sure that you are looking straight ahead with your back straight and are elevated on the balls of your feet (half tiptoed). The most important thing to remember during this exercise is to keep your thighs parallel to the ground.

Next, hop or bounce in the seated position between 3-5 inches per hop, keeping your thighs parallel to the ground. This means you are jumping and landing in the same seated position. Jumping into the air and landing completes 1 repetition.

At the completion (the last rep) of the required set, blast off as high as you possibly can. For example, if you are required to do 1 set of 15 repetitions, you will do 14 squat hops (3-5 inches per jump) and on the 15th squat hop, you will blast off as high as you possibly can.

Squat Hops

| START STANDING | SQUAT TO SITTING | HOP 3-5 INCHES | REPEAT HOPS | BLAST OFF ON LAST REP |

Here is a video of squat hops in action:
https://goo.gl/znGFyr

Optional Exercises

The two optional exercises are sprinting and leg curls. You should do at least one of these exercises to strengthen your hamstrings.

Sprinting

Sprinting as hard as you can is a good way to strengthen your hamstrings and increase your sprinting speed.

Complete ten, 50 yard sprints, two times per week.

Leg Curls

Leg curls are another great exercise for strengthening your ham strings. Leg curl machines can be found at your local gym and school weight room. For this exercise use a weight that is not too light, but which you can still complete comfortably about ten times.

Complete three sets of 10 reps, two times per week.

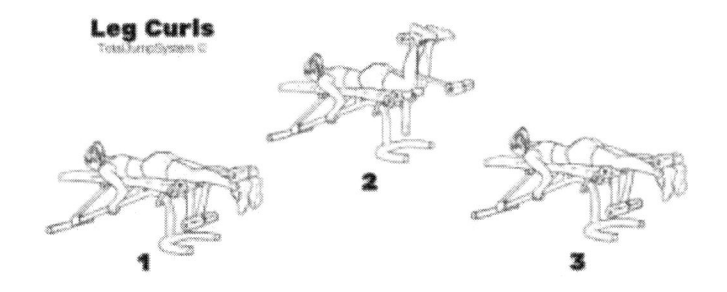

Cool Down Stretching

For this part, you are going to repeat the stretching exercises mentioned before to cool your muscles down. Remember to thoroughly stretch your calves, thighs, hamstring, and back. This "cool down stretching" increases flexibility, prevents cramps, and will minimize soreness.

Chapter 5: Measuring Progress

Measure your vertical leap once a week before you start your workout schedule to determine your progress. You should measure your leap after you've warmed up and stretched.

To measure your vertical leap stand flat footed, reach as high as you can and make a mark with chalk or pencil on a wall. Then take one step and jump off both legs as high as you can into the air, making another mark at the top of your jump. The distance between these two marks is your current vertical leap.

In order for you to fully develop your jumping and overall athletic skills, you must participate in your sport regularly. As long as you do this, you'll maintain about 95% of your vertical jump increase without having to go back and use this program again.

If however you are not active in your sport, you'll need to continue to use this program 3 times a week, using the routines from week 7 in order to maintain your vertical jump increase.

***Note: I wrote this book in an effort to help athletes become better athletes and excel at their sport. Reviews on Amazon are the backbone of books. If this book has helped you, please leave a 5 star review on Amazon. If for any reason you are not satisfied with this book, before leaving any type of negative review on Amazon, please email me at trevor@unknownwealth.com so we can work out a resolution.

CONCLUSION

By believing in yourself, having the desire to succeed, and following the Total Jump System, you will be amazed by your true athletic potential. Work hard and you shall succeed. In order for this program to work, you have to stick with it and motivate yourself to do it. It might be a little boring, but you will thank yourself when you are done!

I hope you enjoyed the program and are on your way to jumping higher than ever! The workout chart and progress chart are located below. Good luck in your athletic pursuits.

NOTE: The **workout chart and **progress chart** are located on the next two pages. Use them as a guide for when to do the recommended exercises, and to record your progress.

Week	Days	Hop Ups Sets	Hop Ups Reps	Calf Raises Sets	Calf Raises Reps	Step Ups Sets	Step Ups Reps	Spring Ups Sets	Spring Ups Reps	Jumpouts Sets	Jumpouts Reps	Squat Hops (Wednesday Only) Sets	Squat Hops (Wednesday Only) Reps
1	M-W-F	2	20	2	10	2	10	2	15	1	100	4	15
2	M-W-F	3	20	2	15	2	15	2	20	1	200	4	20
3	M-W-F	3	25	2	20	2	15	2	25	1	300	4	20
4	M-W-F	3	30	2	25	2	20	2	30	2	200	4	20
5	M-W-F	4	25	2	30	2	20	2	35	2	250	4	25
6	M-W-F	2	50	2	35	2	25	2	40	2	300	4	30
7	M-W-F	4	30	2	40	2	25	2	50	2	350	5	25
8	M-W-F	3	50	2	45	2	30	2	60	4	200	5	25
9	M-W-F	4	50	2	50	2	30	2	70	3	300	5	30
10	M-W-F	5	40	2	55	2	35	2	80	4	250	5	30
11	M-W-F	6	50	4	30	2	35	2	90	4	275	5	30
12	M-W-F	4	75	4	35	2	40	2	100	4	300	6	30
13	Rest Week	Do not do Total Jump System during this week. It is very important to rest your legs during week 13.											
14	M-W-F	3	30	2	30	2	20	2	30	1	250	4	20
15	M-T-W-F	4	100	4	50	2	50	2	100	4	400	5	50

Total Jump System - Page 37

Week	1	2	3	4	5	6	7	8	9	10	11	12	13	14	15
Date															
Height															

Printed in Great Britain
by Amazon